GEL
CANDLES

Creative & Beautiful Candles to Make

CHRIS RANKIN

A Division of Sterling Publishing Co., Inc.
New York

Editor: **Dawn Cusick**

Photo Styling and Book Design: **Theresa Gwynn**

Photography: **Evan Bracken, Richard Hasselberg**

Production Assistance: **Megan Kirby**

Editorial Assistance: **Marcianne Miller, Megan Kirby, Rosemary Kast**

Proofreading: **Susan Carroll**

Library of Congress Cataloging-in-Publication Data

Rankin, Chris.
    Gel candles : creative & beautiful candles to make / Chris Rankin.
        p. cm.
    Includes index.
    ISBN 1-57990-216-2 (pbk.)
    1-57990-234-0 (hbk.)
    1. Candlemaking. I. Title.

TT896.5 .R36 2001
745.593'32—dc21

                                00-050699

10 9 8 7 6 5 4 3

**Published by Lark Books, a division of
Sterling Publishing Co., Inc.**
387 Park Avenue South, New York, N.Y. 10016

© 2001, Lark Books

Distributed in Canada by Sterling Publishing,
c/o Canadian Manda Group, One Atlantic Ave., Suite 105
Toronto, Ontario, Canada M6K 3E7

Distributed in the U.K. by Guild of Master Craftsman Publications Ltd., Castle Place,
166 High Street,
Lewes, East Sussex, England BN7 1XU
Tel: (+ 44) 1273 477374, Fax: (+ 44) 1273 478606, Email:
pubs@thegmcgroup.com, Web: www.gmcpublications.com

Distributed in Australia by Capricorn Link (Australia) Pty Ltd.,
P.O. Box 704, Windsor, NSW 2756 Australia

The written instructions, photographs, designs, patterns, and projects in this volume are intended for the personal use of the reader and may be reproduced for that purpose only. Any other use, especially commercial use, is forbidden under law without written permission of the copyright holder.

Every effort has been made to ensure that all the information in this book is accurate. However, due to differing conditions, tools, and individual skills, the publisher cannot be responsible for any injuries, losses, and other damages that may result from the use of the information in this book.

If you have questions or comments about this book, please contact:
Lark Books
50 College St.
Asheville, NC 28801
(828) 253-0467

*Manufactured in Hong Kong by
Dai Nippon*

ISBN 1-57990-216-2-PB

Contents

Introduction

Finding the right craft can be a lot like finding the right pair of jeans: You have to try on a lot of pairs of them before you find one that fits your budget and your individual style. If you're new to gel candle crafting, rest assured this isn't a craft that will leave you frustrated and disappointed with a closet full of rejects. This is a craft that will showcase your creativity in dozens of unique and wonderful ways. Your candles will decorate your home, dazzle friends and relatives as gifts, and add to the excitement of special celebrations.

Gel candles are wonderfully practical. They last much longer than traditional wax candles, and emit a soft, glowing light as they burn. The gel itself is a pleasure to work with. It melts easily, is fairly inexpensive, and can be enhanced with color, fragrance, and a variety of decorative items. The clear, transparent quality of the gel gives it an eye-catching appeal that will quickly endear itself to you. The techniques are easy to learn: Just melt the gel, pour it into a container, and add a wick. If you're unhappy with the results, remelt the gel and try again.

For gel candle makers, inspiration is everywhere. Great containers can be found in thrift shops, department stores, yard sales, grocery stores, and even your own dish cabinet. Hosting a gel candle does not damage a container, so if your great-great grandmother's cherished tea cup begs to become a gel candle, go for it. Just remove the gel and clean the container when you're done with the candle. For color ideas, tint the gel to match your favorite couch pillow, your wallpaper, or even the exact color of your favorite summer flower. Or pour the gel in layers for a multi-colored effect.

When inspiration wanes, you can make a candle that mimics something from your everyday life (a martini, a frothy beer, an aquarium, even a birthday cake), or make use of a host of special effects to create distinctive themed candles.

Making gel candles will easily be one of the most satisfying crafts you will ever try. Enjoy!

—Chris Rankin

The Basics of Making Gel Candles

Rest assured, you can make a decent gel candle just by following the brief instructions that come with your purchased gel. If you have more than a spark of creative spirit in you, though, you want to make more than "decent" candles—you want to make spectacular gel candles. The tips and techniques in this chapter will guide you to success. Learn how to choose the right container, how to create custom colors, how to cause or prevent bubbles, and how to create special effects.

THE GEL

The gel is sold in solid form in most craft stores. The most challenging part about making gel candles may well be getting the gel out of the container you buy it in. You can start with a genteel approach, if you like, and try removing it with a large spoon. Solid gel can be difficult to cut through with a spoon, though, and this may cause more frustration than it's worth. A better strategy is to dig right in with your bare hands. Once you remove the first few clumps, the rest of the gel usually comes out in a large, easy-to-manage piece.

MELTING

At first you'll be impressed with how quickly the gel melts. Once your first impression wears off, though, you will undoubtedly get impatient. Your container is all ready and your creative juices are flowing, and you're sick of waiting. You'll be tempted to speed the process along by turning up the heat. Or you may be tempted to leave the gel unattended while you do a quick chore in another room or answer the phone. Don't! The gel can reach its flash point (the point at which it combusts into flames) very quickly. Review the safety precautions on page 8 before you make your first candle.

You can melt enough gel to make just one candle or you can melt a large batch for multiple candles. Melting a large quantity of gel can take a surprisingly long time, so take extra note of the advice in the paragraph above. Note: The melted gel cools very quickly, so if you're pouring multiple candles from a single batch of gel and want them all to have the same amount (or lack) of bubbles, be sure to check the gel's temperature before pouring each new candle.

You should heat the gel in a pan over low heat and not exceed the temperature recommended by the gel's manufacturer. Be sure to read the label every time—different manufacturers use slightly different gels so the safe temperature can vary a lot. Avoid the temptation to melt the gel in the microwave. It doesn't work and can cause personal injury.

HOW HOT IS IT?

If you're like most people, a number on a thermometer doesn't mean much. If the gel is in a liquid state, it will hurt when it touches your skin. If it's hot enough, the gel can give you a significant burn. Unlike an ordinary burn where the heat exposure is shortened by your reflexes, you can't move your hand (or other part of your body) away from the gel to get away from the heat. The gel sticks to the skin and keeps on burning. Translation: You can't be too careful when working with liquid gel.

Liquid gel is also hot enough to melt a plastic ladle or spoon, but not hot enough to ignite a paper towel if you use it as a spoon rest.

ESTIMATING QUANTITY

There's no perfect way to estimate quantity unless you know the exact volume of your candle container and the precise amount of gel you've purchased (in ounces or liters) from the manufacturer. Just visualize the space and add some extra for comfort. There's never any harm in overestimating—just return the excess gel to the original container after it hardens and use it for the next candle.

RECYCLING

One of the best things about gel candles is how recyclable they are. If you tire of the yellow gel candle that sits at your bedside, just melt the gel, add a touch of blue dye, and voila—you have a new green candle. Both the gel and the containers can be reused as many times as you like. (The only time you can't re-melt the candle gel is when you've been careless about trimming the wick [see page 11] and there's a lot of soot in your gel.)

TOOLS AND SUPPLIES

An ordinary cooking pan is needed to melt the solid gel. You can use one of your everyday pots and just scrub it well with a grease-dissolving dish detergent after each use, or you can purchase an inexpensive pot that's reserved just for making gel candles.

A clip-on pan thermometer is necessary to help you keep a close watch on the gel's

SAFETY

IF YOU'RE TEMPTED TO SKIP THIS SECTION, PLEASE DON'T!

It's easy to get carried away in the creative excitement of making a candle and forget about how hot the gel is. If you receive a gel burn, immediately treat the burned area with ice and follow up with medical care if necessary. Following are some important tips to keep in mind as you work with gel.

• **Always be prepared** for the worst. If you overheat your gel and it ignites, remember that it's an oil fire and should be treated accordingly. DO NOT PUT WATER ON THE FIRE. For small fires, immediately put the lid on the pan and remove the pan from the heat source. For larger fires, douse with baking soda or use a kitchen fire extinguisher.

• **Wear protective eyewear** for splatters, especially when you're working with large batches of gel.

• **Keep well-fitting hand protection** within easy reach of your work area.

• **Make sure your pan is centered** in the middle of the burner. If you see that your pan of melted gel is about to slide off the burner, don't try to save it—just get out of the way.

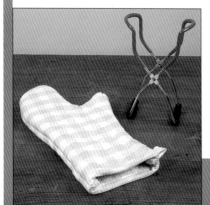

• **Keep children and pets out of the kitchen** when working with liquid gel.

• **Remind older children** that the gel is not edible (even though the finished candles may look like their favorite dessert). For younger children, treat the candles like prescription medication: Keep them out of reach and call a Poison Control center immediately if you suspect a child has eaten one.

• **Don't burn the candles** for more than a few hours at a time.

• **Don't leave** a burning candle unattended.

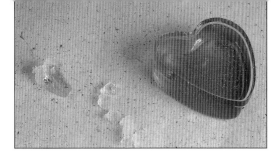

temperature. This is not a tool to do without. Two-hundred-degree F melted gel (93°C), which is perfectly safe, looks exactly the same as 300°F (149°C) melted gel, which could cause a flash fire at any moment.

A metal spoon is helpful for stirring the gel as it melts. Wood spoons are not recommended because they can cause excess bubbling.

THE COOLING PROCESS

Depending on the size of your container and the temperature of your gel when you poured it, the gel will solidify in a few hours or less. If you don't mind a few bubbles, you can allow your gel candle to cool anywhere it won't be disturbed. For faster cooling or to help prevent bubbles, place the candle in the refrigerator. It's hard to resist touching the gel as it cools, so it's likely you may end up with fingerprint marks on the top of your candle. To get rid of them, just heat the candle in a 175°F (79°C) oven until the gel melts, then stir well and try the cooling process again.

THE MESS FACTOR

There's good news and bad news about cleaning up after a session of gel candle making. The good news: Removing leftover gel from the bottom of a pan or a container is a snap. It usually peels away in one large piece. The bad news: Small pieces of gel are not easy to clean up. In fact, you will find them in all kinds of unexpected and amazing places. The family pet's fur, your windows, your shoelaces, and even on your computer's mouse pad are just a few of the many possibilities. The main thing to remember about these smaller pieces is that a large portion of their volume is made up of mineral oil, so however innocent they look, they can leave blotchy oil stains on clothing, carpets, and paper. To remove the stains from clothing, pretreat the stains the same way you would a butter or salad dressing stain.

Do your best to prevent the gel, even small amounts, from getting on your stove top burners. The gel quickly blends in with the burner, and then the next time you use the stove, the

Small pieces of gel (left) can be a clean-up challenge, while larger pieces (right) are easy to maneuver.

gel will release enough smoke to set off the smoke alarm. Burner spills happen most frequently after you've poured the melted gel into your container and a small amount of gel runs down the sides of the pan without notice.

CONTAINERS

One of the unique and wonderful things about gel candles is that the container will show in your finished candle. (Compare to traditional wax candles, in which the container serves only as a mold.) This feature opens the door to a world of creativity.

PREPARATION

Clean and dry your containers very well before using. Soap residue, oils, and glue from stickers can all interact with your gel and cause unpleasant side effects.

DECISIONS, DECISIONS

Look for imaginative containers in antique stores, thrift shops, and even around your home. Following is a short list of some ideas to get you started.

Everyday glassware makes great containers for gel candles. Consider fishbowls, flower vases, and interesting jars.

Drinking glasses of any type—beer mugs, martini glasses, etc.—make novel and fun gel candles.

Colored glass containers are a great option, especially for those who

don't feel confident in their abilities to get an exact color using gel dyes.

Decorated glass containers can be found in great variety at low cost in many home decor stores. Etched and painted glass containers are good choices.

Antique containers are safe to use for gel containers. When you tire of the candle, just remove the leftover gel and clean the container with mineral spirits.

Cylinders can make striking gel candles. Several things should be kept in mind when using them, though. First, they tend to cause wells in the gel, with larger wells forming in the narrowest cylinders. If the candle is for

personal use, who cares? It will have a well in it as soon as you burn it anyway. If the candle is a gift, however, you may want to pour another layer to fill the well or choose a different type of container.

WICKS

Wicks are the silent heroes of every candle. If they're chosen and placed correctly, no one will give them a second thought, and they'll give you hours of splendid beauty.

VARIETIES

A decent selection of candle wicking can be found at most craft stores. For gel candles, you have several choices. Zinc-cored wicks are stiff and burn well, as do wax-coated wicks. Do not use paper wicks in gel candles. Tabbed wicks are also available, providing you with an easy way to anchor the wick in the bottom of your candle container. Wicks also come in an assortment of sizes that should be chosen with care according to the size of your container. Refer to the wick manufacturer's instructions for guidance.

WICK PREPARATION & PLACEMENT

You have several choices in positioning your wick in a gel candle container. If you don't mind a few bubbles in your gel candle (the gel reacts with the glue and causes bubbling), the easiest thing to do is to choose a pretabbed wick and hot-glue the tab to the bottom of the container. Roll the excess wick around a wooden cooking skewer or a pencil and pour the gel.

Yet another option is to pour the gel first and then arrange the wick. If you're after a bubble-free candle, dip the wick in some melted gel and leave it there until the gel stops bubbling. Remove the wick, wait a minute, and then run your fingers down the wick to remove the excess gel. Roll the top of the wick around a wooden cooking skewer or pencil and position it over the container.

TAMING REBELLIOUS WICKS

You'll be saddened to learn that even the most perfectly placed wick can wander off track as your gel candle cools. If this happens, you have two choices. You can live with it (who cares if it's a little crooked?), or you can fix it. Fortunately for the Type As among us, fixing an errant wick is as simple as placing

the candle in a 175°F (79°C) oven until the gel melts and then repositioning it.

WICK MAINTENANCE

Trimming the wick to $\frac{1}{4}$ inch (6 mm) is just as important as watering your houseplants or changing your car oil. A wick that's much taller than $\frac{1}{4}$ inch is a potential safety hazard because the increased flame size could generate enough heat to ignite the gel. If safety issues don't get your attention, take a few minutes to study the candle at right. When the wick goes untrimmed, a soot residue accumulates in the melted gel pool and ruins the beauty of the candle. To trim a wick, simply turn the candle upside down and trim with a pair of small scissors or nail clippers.

SAFETY

It's very important to not burn the wick all the way down to the bottom of the container. If you're using pretabbed wicks, the metal tab will keep you honest. If you're not using metal tabs, cut the wick to at least an inch (2.5 cm) shorter than the height of the container. It's also important to trim the wick regularly. (See below.)

SHORT WICKS

In some instances, a short wick is the ideal choice for safety or aesthetic reasons. Use the examples below as a guide. Keep in mind that "short" is a relative term. If you're using a 10-inch-tall (25 cm) container, a short wick might be 4 inches (10 cm). If you're using a 3-inch-tall (7.5 cm) container, a short wick might be 1 inch.

• When you're using a container with a narrow (less than 2 inches, 5 cm) opening, it makes sense to use a short wick. The chances that a gel puddle will come in prolonged contact with the edge of the container are fairly good with narrow containers, even if you choose the smallest width wick available. Also, trimming the wick to the $\frac{1}{4}$ inch necessary to prevent soot buildup becomes close to impossible when

Above: An example of a candle whose wick was not trimmed to $\frac{1}{4}$ inch (6 mm) after every use.

Below: A short wick held in place on a cooking skewer.

Left: An assortment of commercially available wicks.

An errant wick doesn't ruin the beauty of this gel candle.

you're trying to get scissors or clippers into the opening of a narrow container.

• When you plan to embed items in the gel that may be flammable, a short wick can be strategically placed to prevent any chance that the wick's flame (or a hot gel pool) would be anywhere near the flammable items.

• When you're planning a candle in which a perfectly straight wick is critical to the design, it's much safer to use a short wick. Candles made with untinted gel in transparent containers or candles made in very tall containers tend to do better with short wicks because a long wick with even a slight bend to it is very obvious in the finished candle.

COLOR

Sometimes just a hint of color is the perfect choice for a gel candle; other gel candle designs call for bright, vibrant colors. An adventuresome spirit is all you really need to get great color results. Remember, if you don't like the color, it takes only a few minutes to recycle the gel and try again.

USING DYES

Dyes made especially for gel candles are available, but you can also use dyes made for wax candles. Do not use food coloring.

To add the dye, heat your gel until it is completely liquefied, then stir in small amounts of dye until you're happy with the color. (A small grater can be a big help if you're using solid dyes.) A good way to check the color is to place a spoonful of the tinted gel on a sheet of heavy white paper. Allow the gel to solidify, then see how you like the color. If the color appears too dark, simply dilute it by melting more clear gel in your

pan. If the color appears too light, simply add a little more dye.

Always save any leftover scraps of colored gel. Just remove the hardened gel from the bottom of the pan or container and store it in a sealable plastic bag. You can use these scraps like dyes, either adding them to other colors to form subtle color variations or melting them down to be used as is.

WAX CANDLE CHUNKS

Wax chunks are a great way to add color and shape to your candles. You can buy them in precut shapes or cut your own from leftover scraps donated by your favorite wax candle-maker. (The candle on page 54 features wax chunks in bright colors that resemble a bowl of fresh fruit when arranged in a gel candle.)

When working with wax chunks, always remember to heat your gel to the highest temperature recommended by the gel's manufacturer, then allow the gel to cool for a few minutes before pouring. (Pouring hot gel over wax chunks can cause them to melt on the edges, which makes the wax colors look like they're bleeding into the clear gel.)

COLORED SAND

Craft sands come in a great variety of colors. Use the sand in thick or thin layers, either as a design element (see the candles on pages 64

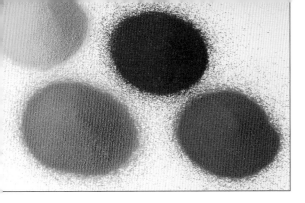

and 65) or as accents for scenic candles such as those on pages 18 and 70. There are several tricks to working successfully with craft sand. First, if you plan to make a candle with alternating layers of gel and sand, be sure to allow each layer of gel to completely solidify before adding a layer of sand. If you try to hurry the process, you will be punished with sagging gel. The other trick is to take extra care to make sure that any errant drops of gel that may have run down the inside of the container are removed before adding a layer of sand. Otherwise, several hundred sand granules will cling to the gel and ruin the clean lines of your candle. Remember, also, that you aren't limited to the commercially produced sand colors. Any color can be lightened by mixing with beach sand and new colors can be created by mixing several colors together. Also, keep in mind that the sand color in the finished candle will usually look several shades darker than it does in the package.

SPECIAL EFFECTS

FRAGRANCE

Fragrance adds a wonderful dimension to gel candles, but it should be added with care. For aesthetic reasons, you need to choose a fragrance oil that is compatible with the gel. The wrong fragrance oil will cause your gel to cloud as it cools. Another consideration is flash point. Because most fragrance oils will ignite at a much lower temperature than the gel, you should use only a drop or two of fragrance oils for an average-sized candle. More than that and the entire surface of the gel may ignite when you light the wick. Several gel manufacturers also make a line of gel-compatible fragrances. If you're ordering fragrance from another source, be sure to ask if it will be compatible with the mineral-oil-based gel. When making fragrant candles, it's a good idea to start with the assumption that they may well ignite: Watch them carefully and do not leave them unattended. Add the fragrance oil just before you pour the gel and stir well.

LAYERS

You can create all kinds of interesting looks by pouring different colors of gel on top of each other. Tint and pour the gel as you would for a regular candle, allowing each layer to completely solidify before pouring the next. Getting a bubble-free layered look can be virtually impossible, though, because the anti-bubble techniques on page 15 can't be used when working with layers.

OPAQUENESS

Although gel candles are known for their clear, translucent quality, there may be times when you prefer a more opaque look. There are two main ways to achieve this look. The first is to tint the gel with crayon shavings instead of candle dye. The second is to repeatedly fold the gel over as it cools with a butter knife. Transfer the gel to the container when it starts to become too stiff to handle.

EMBEDS

The ability to embed objects in a gel candle is one of this craft's best features. It takes some practice to master the techniques, though, so put your perfectionist personality in the closet for a while and remember that you can put the entire candle in the oven, melt it back down (175°F, 79°C for several hours), and try again if necessary.

Above: Gel layers are easy to create—just pour each layer one at a time and allow them to completely cool between pours.

Below: An opaque gel candle created by tinting the gel with a small amount of shaved crayon.

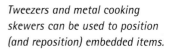

Be sure to keep safety in mind when choosing items to embed. If you're tempted to use flammable items in a gel candle, use a short wick that will never burn near these items. Generally, items made from too much water or too much oxygen will bubble up and disintigrate in the gel. (Remember making volcanoes from vinegar and baking soda in junior high science classes?) Following is a list of possible items to embed.

Ceramic, metal, or glass items are fun to arrange for decorative effect in gel candles. The possibilities here are virtually endless. You can find interesting objects in your jewelry box, old drawers, craft stores, or in shops that specialize in miniatures for dollhouses or toy trains.

Marbles, glass pebbles, and beads also make great choices for gel embeds. They come in a wonderful variety of sizes, colors, and shapes, and it's easy to design a gel candle around your favorite finds. Place them on the bottom of the container before pouring the gel or drop them in one at a time after the gel has thickened.

Silk flowers and foliage make wonderful additions to gel candles. Use a good pair of wire cutters to remove the stem close to the back of the flower so that it can sit flush against the side or bottom of the candle's container.

Paper, photocopies, and photographs can be added to your gel candles. Position them against one of the inside walls of your container and pour the gel as you normally would. Be sure to place the wick well away from all paper products.

Tweezers and metal cooking skewers are the tools of success when working with embeds. Use them to place the items before your pour the gel and to reposition wandering embeds after you've poured the gel.

Tweezers and metal cooking skewers can be used to position (and reposition) embedded items.

When you want your embeds to be in an exact place in the finished candle, it's best to suspend them in the container with sewing thread. If the item has a place where you can string the thread, such as a Christmas ornament or a bead, this is a quick and easy task. For items such as ceramic animals, you will need to suspend the items over two or three rows of string, as though you're making them a hammock to rest in. After the gel in your candle has finished solidifying, you can remove the strings by gently tugging on them.

BUBBLES

Bubbles are nebulous creatures, always showing up and leaving when you least expect them. You can go to bed with a perfectly clear gel candle and wake up to discover hundreds of bubbles where there were none. Try to avoid choosing camps over the bubble issue. In a simple candle with nothing embedded in it, bubbles can transform a plain candle into a stunning one, plus they capture the light and glow when the candle's lit. Bubbles are also nice to have around when they tie in with a candle's design theme, such as an aquarium candle or a beer stein candle.

CONQUERING BUBBLES

Virtually all bubbles are caused by one of three things: the heating temperature of the gel, reactions between the gel and items in your candle, and pouring the gel. If you really want bubble-free gel candles, you will need an arsenal of bubble-ridding techniques at your fingertips. Use one or all of the tips that follow, depending on your patience level and your willingness to experiment.

Heat your container for at least 10 minutes in a 175°F oven (79°C) before pouring the gel. Preheating the container is an easy step to integrate into your candlemaking routine: Just put the container in the oven right after you put your gel on the stove-top. Be sure to use hand protection during removal and as you pour the gel because the glass will be hot.

Heat the gel to the highest temperature recommended by the gel's manufacturer. Generally, the higher the pour temperature, the fewer the bubbles. When heating gel to high temperatures, always keep a close watch on the gel because just a few minutes' of distraction can easily cause a grease fire. Also, when pouring multiple candles, keep a close watch on the thermometer. You may have poured the first candle at a high temperature, but the gel temperature for subsequent candles can easily be 50 degrees F (10°C) less if the pan was removed from the heat.

Pretreat all ceramic, glass, and metallic items that you plan to embed in a gel candle by placing them in a pan with a small amount of melted gel. Watch the items carefully for bubbles. If no bubbles appear, use tweezers to carefully remove the items, holding them over the pan until the gel solidifies. If the items do bubble, leave them in the gel until they stop, stirring occasionally. If an item continues to bubble for more than a few minutes, look for a replacement unless you're willing to have bubbles in the finished candle.

Avoid using items made with large amounts of glue. The glue often reacts with the gel and bubbles excessively.

If possible, pour the gel at an angle, as you would a beer, to minimize bubbling.

Presoak your wicks in some melted gel and watch for bubbling. When the bubbling stops, lift the wick out, wait 30 seconds, and then run your fingers down the wick to remove excess gel.

Stir your newly poured gel with a bubble stick. Plastic bubble sticks can be found in almost all stores that carry canning supplies. Just place the stick in the gel and gently stir it through the gel in a swirling motion.

Place newly poured candles in the refrigerator as soon as possible and leave them undisturbed for several hours. Safety note: The heat from the gel can make the glass very hot, so use hand protection and make sure the path is clear as you move the candle from the stove-top to the refrigerator.

Doublecheck the temperature before pouring the gel, especially if you're pouring more than one candle from the same batch of gel. Just a few minutes between pours can produce twice as many bubbles.

If all else fails, bake your finished candles for several hours in a 175°F (79°C) oven until the bubbles are gone. Stir well with a bubble stick and cool the candle in the refrigerator. This process can be repeated several times.

Above, top: The bubbles in these candles are welcome additions. They enhance an otherwise plain candle (left) and add realism to a faux champagne candle (right).

Above: The abundant bubbles in this candle obstruct the embedded swans. The candle should be remade to remove the bubbles.

Below: A few swirls with an inexpensive bubble stick help remove air bubbles from gel candles before they cool.

Everyday
Candles

Gel candles can easily become a

special part of your everyday decor.

Display them on nightstands, around

the bath tub, as centerpieces, on coffee

tables, or anywhere else that strikes

your fancy. Although shopping for

unique glass containers can be a lot of

fun, don't overlook the containers that

may already be in your home. Wine

glasses, serving bowls, flower vases,

and antique containers are just a few

of the possibilities.

Garden Candle

You don't need a green thumb to make this gracious gift candle for your favorite gardener. It's also a perfect housewarming gift, especially for young homeowners facing their first garden.

MATERIALS

- Clip-on pan thermometer
- Pan
- Small glass flowerpot
- Garden-themed ceramic miniatures (potted flowers, a shovel, and a watering can were used here)
- Sewing thread
- Green craft sand
- Candle gel
- Wick

INSTRUCTIONS

1 Melt a small amount of gel in a small pan. Place the watering can (or other item you wish to place at the top of the candle) in the gel and watch for bubbles. If no bubbles appear, use tweezers to remove the can by its handle, holding it over the pan until the gel solidifies. If the watering can does bubble, leave it in the gel until it stops bubbling, stirring occasionally.

2 Line the bottom of the flowerpot with a layer of green sand. Pour a thin layer of gel over the sand. Suspend the watering can in the container and secure by taping the string in place. Place the remaining miniatures in the gel and repeat Step 1.

3 Melt enough gel to fill the container over low heat until it reaches the highest temperature recommended by the manufacturer. Pour the liquid gel over the miniatures and arrange a wick, then place in the refrigerator for several hours to cool. *Note: If your finished candle has more bubbles in it than you like, place it in a 175°F (79°C) oven for several hours, then stir out any remaining bubbles with the bubble stick and cool again in the refrigerator.*

4 Remove the strings from the finished candle by gently pulling on them.

Designer: **Theresa Gwynn**

Seashore Gel Candle

Underwater scenes are ideally suited to gel candles, especially with bubbles that create the feeling of depth and movement. This small fishbowl candle is a lovely memory catcher if you fill it with shells collected from your seaside vacation. Display it with larger shells and pebbles and sun-drenched photos.

MATERIALS

- Clip-on pan thermometer
- Pan
- Small fishbowl
- Beach sand
- Assorted shells in varying sizes
- Candle gel
- Gel dye
- Wick
- Metal skewer

INSTRUCTIONS

1 Line the bottom of your container with beach sand. Melt a small amount of gel in a small pan and pour it over the sand, then arrange the shells in the gel.

2 Melt a small amount of gel over low heat to the highest temperature recommended by the manufacturer. Add just enough blue to lightly tint the gel. (Doublecheck the color by removing a small amount of gel on a spoon and placing it on a sheet of heavy white paper.) Add additional gel to the pan if the color is too dark or additional dye if it's too light.

3 Arrange the wick and place the container in the refrigerator for several hours. A few bubbles are an attractive addition to this candle, but if your finished candle has more bubbles in it than you like, place it in a 175°F (79°C) oven for several hours, then stir out any remaining bubbles with the bubble stick and cool again in the refrigerator.

Designers: **Theresa Gwynn** *(left) and* **Megan Kirby** *(right)*

VARIATION

Pour lightly tinted gel into a large seashell and add a short wick.

Very Simple Votive Candles

*S*hhh...these candles are so stunning—especially if they're displayed in a group—it's a shame to reveal how easy they are to make! Use any holder design with bold lines and open space to accentuate the translucent beauty of the gel candles.

MATERIALS

- Clip-on pan thermometer
- Pan
- Interesting glass votive candle holders
- Candle gel
- Gel dye and/or fragrance
- Wick

INSTRUCTIONS

1 Melt enough gel to fill the container over low heat. For lots of bubbles, pour the gel as soon as it melts. For fewer bubbles, refer to the antibubble suggestions on pages 14 and 15. Stir in a small amount of gel dye and/or fragrance oil. Pour the gel and arrange a short wick (about 1 inch, 2.5 cm).

Designer: **Chris Rankin** *(left and right)*

Safety Note: *Be sure to note the information on page 13 about adding fragrance to gel candles.*

VARIATION

Many votive candle holders come in colored and cut glass. These candles are just as simple to make, but admirers will never guess how simple they are to make.

Gold Leaf Centerpiece

The unique shape of this glass container and the striking effect of the gold leaves combine to make this candle a centerpiece attraction. Surround it with real leaves to increase its dramatic effect.

MATERIALS

- Clip-on pan thermometer
- Pan
- Glass container
- Candle gel
- Gel dye
- Wick
- Gold, nonflammable leaves
- Plastic jelly stick
- Metal skewer

INSTRUCTIONS

1 Melt a small amount of gel in a pan over low heat to the highest temperature recommended by the manufacturer. Add the dye in small amounts until the gel is a pale green. (Doublecheck the color by removing a small amount of gel on a spoon and placing it on a sheet of heavy white paper.) Add additional gel to the pan if the color is too dark or additional dye if it's too light.

2 Dip the leaves in the gel and set them aside. Position the wick and pour the gel into the container. Allow the gel to set for several minutes, then arrange the leaves around the edges of the container, using the skewer to guide them into place and taking care to avoid close contact with the wick. Gently stir the gel with the plastic bubble stick, then allow the gel to solidify undisturbed for several hours.

Designer: **Terry Taylor** *(left and right)*

VARIATION

Lightly glue colorful beach glass shards to the sides of a container and fill with gel. *Note: The glue often reacts with the gel and causes bubbles, and it's virtually impossible to suspend the shards with string, so don't attempt this candle if you despise bubbles.*

Shaped Wire Gel Candles

Spirals have been used by ancient peoples in all parts of the globe to remind them of the recurring cycles of life. Viking explorers painted spirals on their ships to symbolize their inevitable struggles against sun and waves and wind—and their eventual return home. In hot-red wire spirals, this gel candle sends a timeless message: "'Bon voyage' and hurry home..."

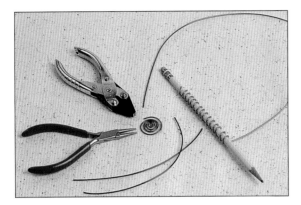

MATERIALS

- Clip-on pan thermometer
- Pan
- Large wine glass
- Candle gel
- Wick
- 20-gauge colored wire
- Wire cutters
- Jewelry pliers
- Metal skewer
- Bubble stick

INSTRUCTIONS

1 Cut the wire into half a dozen 8-inch (20 cm) lengths. For each spiral, wrap one end of the wire around the nose of the jewelry pliers to form a loop. Curve the wire around the loop until you have a good-sized spiral. Cut off any excess wire. Repeat with the other wire lengths.

2 String each spiral onto a length of string and suspend the spirals in varying locations over the container.

3 Melt the gel over low heat in a pan until it reaches the highest temperature recommended by the manufacturer. Pour the gel into the glass and position the wick. Allow the gel to solidify undisturbed in the refrigerator for several hours.

4 Remove the strings from the finished candle by gently pulling on them.

Note: If your finished candle has more bubbles in it than you like, place it in a 175°F (79°C) oven for several hours, then stir out any remaining bubbles with the bubble stick and cool again in the refrigerator.

Designer: **Terry Taylor** *(left and right)*

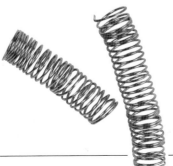

VARIATION

Instead of wire spirals, shape the wire into long springs by wrapping 10-inch (25 cm) lengths around a pencil.

Teatime

Teacups make wonderful containers for gel candles and can be embellished with mosaic chips (use a chipped plate from your favorite china setting for a matching candle) or a tinted gel and teaspoon. Note: Glass tea settings can be found in antique stores and bargain basements for a pittance, and such treasure-hunting trips will undoubtedly give you ideas for other novel gel candle containers.

MATERIALS

- Clip-on pan thermometer
- Pan
- Small ceramic plate with motif
- Tile nippers
- Safety glasses
- Clear glass teacup and saucer
- Candle gel
- Wick
- Metal skewer

INSTRUCTIONS

1 Break the plate up into small pieces about 1 inch (2.5 cm) in size using the tile nippers. (Wear safety glasses while you are cutting.)

2 Melt a small amount of gel in a pan over low heat to the highest temperature recommended by the manufacturer. Allow the gel to set for two minutes, then place the plate pieces in the gel. Working quickly, position the mosaic pieces as desired, using the metal skewer to guide them into place. Add the wick and place the candle in an area where it won't be disturbed for several hours.

Designer: **Terry Taylor** *(left and right)*

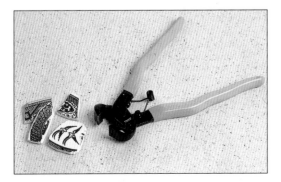

VARIATION

Tint the gel to a fruity red color and place a teaspoon on the side. Add the wick.

Summer Stripes Gel Candles

These playful summer-stripe painted containers need nothing more than clear gel and a wick to cheer up a table. The more brightly colored a container is, the less work it means you have to do to create something wonderful.

MATERIALS

- Clip-on pan thermometer
- Pan
- Painted glass container
- Candle gel
- Wick

INSTRUCTIONS

1 Melt enough gel to fill the container in a pan over low heat. For lots of bubbles, pour the gel as soon as it melts. For fewer bubbles, refer to the antibubble suggestions on pages 14 and 15. Pour the gel and arrange the wick.

Designer Tip: *Avoid the temptation to add dye to gel candles made in painted containers. The clear gel on the interior makes a beautiful contrast to the decorative exterior.*

Designer: **Chris Rankin** *(left and right)*

VARIATION

Make a quick gel candle in a small, painted glass container for any last-minute gift-giving occasion.

Pedestal Gel Candles

Sturdy glass candlesticks, topped with graceful glass containers and filled with brightly colored gel...voila! A new combo that looks perfect together. The bold-colored gel on top balances the dramatic lines of the candlesticks. Use a pale tint for more delicate duos.

MATERIALS

- Clip-on pan thermometer
- Pan
- Pedestal candle stands and hurricanes
- Candle gel
- Gel dye and/or fragrance if desired
- Wick

INSTRUCTIONS

1 Melt enough gel to fill the container in a pan over low heat. For lots of bubbles, pour the gel as soon as it melts. For fewer bubbles, refer to the antibubble suggestions on pages 14 and 15. Pour the gel and arrange a short wick (about an 1 inch, 2.5 cm).

Designers: **Megan Kirby** *(left) and* **Terry Taylor** *(right)*

Safety Note: *Remember to trim your wick to ¹/₄ (6 mm) inch after every use.*

VARIATION

Using different stands is a quick way to completely change the look of these candles. Why not make several sets for easy mix and matching?

Fruit 'n Veggies Gel Candle

So many people are going vegetarian these days, especially on summer nights when salads are the answer to a too-hot kitchen. This clear, cool-looking candle filled with miniature fruits and veggies looks great on a table, no matter what's being served.

INSTRUCTIONS

1 Melt a small amount of gel in a small pan. Place the miniatures in the gel and watch for bubbles. If no bubbles appear, use tweezers to remove them one at a time, holding each one over the pan until the gel solidifies. If the gel around the miniatures does bubble, leave the items in the gel until the bubbling stops, stirring occasionally.

2 Melt enough gel to fill the container over low heat until it reaches the highest temperature recommended by the manufacturer. Pour the liquid gel over the miniatures. Use the metal skewer to rearrange the miniatures if desired. Arrange the wick. Gently swirl the gel with the bubble stick to remove as many bubbles as possible, then place in the refrigerator for several hours to solidify.

Note: If your finished candle has more bubbles in it than you like, place it in a 175°F (79°C) oven for several hours, then stir out any remaining bubbles with the bubble stick and cool again in the refrigerator.

Designers: **Theresa Gwynn** *and* **Terry Taylor**

MATERIALS

- Clip-on pan thermometer
- Pan
- Square glass container
- Kitchen-themed ceramic or metal miniatures (fresh fruits and vegetables were used here)
- Candle gel
- Wick
- Metal skewer
- Bubble stick

Tubular Gels

This "look at me!" cluster of tall glass tubes is so easy to make you'll have a hard time stopping at only four tubes! This one combines tubes of colored gel and beads. Consider other tubes with colored sand, glitter, rhinestones, sequins...the possibilities are endless!

MATERIALS

- Clip-on pan thermometer
- Pan
- Grouping of tall cylinders (this grouping was found in a bead shop)
- Candle gel
- Gel dye
- Wick
- Beads

INSTRUCTIONS

1 Melt the gel over low heat in a pan to the highest temperature recommended by the manufacturer. Add just enough dye to lightly tint the gel. Doublecheck the color by removing a small amount of gel on a spoon and placing it on a sheet of heavy white paper. Add additional gel to the pan if the color is too dark or additional dye if it's too light.

2 Pour the gel into the desired cylinders and add a short wick. Allow to cool in the refrigerator.

3 Repeat Steps 1 and 2 as desired, leaving at least one of the cylinders empty.

4 Fill the empty cylinder(s) with your favorite beads.

Note: Remember that gel candles poured in cylinders tend to develop wells at the top as they cool.

Designer: **Chris Rankin** *(left and right)*

VARIATION

Tall, colorful bud vases make lovely gel candles.

Layered Angles Gel Candle

MATERIALS

o Clip-on pan thermometer
o Pan
o Tall parfait glass
o Candle gel
o Gel dye
o Wick
o Bubble stick

Men will love the strong lines and solid base of this angled candle. It provides a handsome glow to a college dorm or new bachelor pad. The angled layers are easy to achieve: Just pour one layer of gel at a time and tip the container at an angle as the gel cools.

INSTRUCTIONS

1 Melt a small amount of gel in a small pan and add just enough dye to lightly tint it. Doublecheck the color by removing a small amount of gel on a spoon and placing it on a sheet of heavy white paper. Add additional gel to the pan if the color is too dark or additional dye if it's too light.

2 Pour 2 inches (5 cm) of gel into the glass. Gently stir the gel with the bubble stick in a swirling pattern. Place the glass at an angle in the refrigerator and allow the gel to solidify.

3 Repeat Steps 1 and 2 with additional layers of gel in different colors.

4 For the final layer, fill the top few inches of the container with gel, then arrange the wick, stir well with the bubble stick, and place in the refrigerator to solidify.

Designer: **Terry Taylor** *(left) and* **Megan Kirby** *(right)*

Safety Note: *Do not allow the wick to burn within 1 (2.5 cm) inch of the bottom of the container.*

VARIATION

Make a similar candle with straight layers instead of angled ones in parfait glasses.

Etched Glass
Gel Candles

*T*he etched glass container adds an interesting element of texture to this simple candle. Gel is so easy to clean out of a container that it can be used without worry even in valuable antique glass.

MATERIALS

- Clip-on pan thermometer
- Pan
- Etched glass containers
- Candle gel
- Wick
- Gel dye

INSTRUCTIONS

1 Melt the gel over low heat to the highest temperature recommended by the manufacturer. Add the dye in small amounts until you are satisfied with the color. (To doublecheck the color, place a tablespoon of gel on a piece of heavy white paper.) Position the wick and pour the gel. *Note: For containers with an all-over etched pattern like these, bubbles can distract from the beauty of the pattern, so try to prevent them. (See page 15.)*

Designers: **Dawn Cusick** *(left) and* **Theresa Gwynn** *(right)*

VARIATION

An inexpensive bud vase with an etched design makes a beautiful candle when lightly tinted gel is added. For etched patterns like this one, in which some of the container's surface area is left plain, bubbles can be an attractive addition to the finished candle.

Marbles in Glass

A *playful mix of gel and marbles makes this simple design sparkle with color and shape. It's just a glass butter dish with the lid inverted. Any pretty-shaped glass dish-lid duo would do.*

MATERIALS

o Clip-on pan thermometer
o Pan
o Glass butter dish and lid*
o Small marbles in several colors
o Small glass pebbles in a solid color
o Candle gel
o Wick

INSTRUCTIONS

* *The lid will need to lie flat when you invert it; test for flatness before pouring gel!*

1 Line the butter dish with a single layer of marbles. Melt the gel in a pan over low heat to the highest temperature recommended by the manufacturer. Pour the melted gel over the marbles. Position a wick on each end of the candle. Allow the gel to completely solidify without disturbing.

2 Place the candle in the center of the butter dish. Fill the space around the lid with several layers of glass beads. (Beans, confetti, and other materials would make fun variations.)

3 Melt a small amount of gel and pour it over the beads.

Designers: **Theresa Gwynn** *(left) and* **Terry Taylor** *(right)*

VARIATION

For a simple, quick candle, line the bottom of a nice container with several colors of glass pebbles. Fill the container with gel and add a wick.

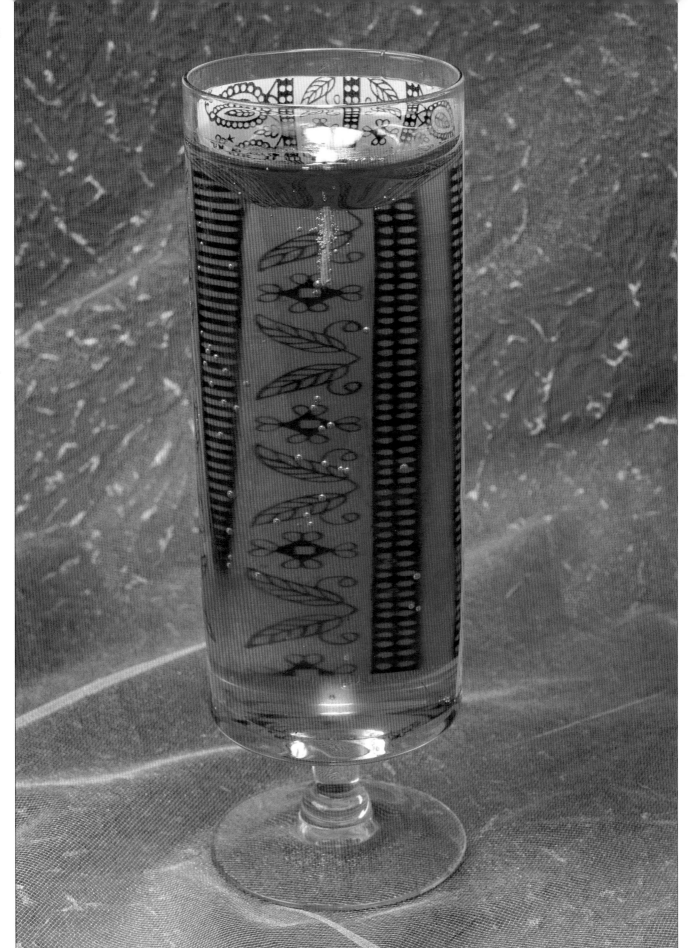

Paper Pattern In Glass

This graceful "Old European" pattern suits the slim height of the glass. Celtic swirls, Egyptian hieroglyphics, and Anasazi geometrics are other attractive patterns that seem to dance when the candle is lit.

MATERIALS

- Clip-on pan thermometer
- Pan
- Glass container with smooth, even curves
- Black-and-white or color photocopy to fit inside the container
- Candle gel
- Wick
- Bubble stick

INSTRUCTIONS

1 Trim the photocopy to fit inside the container and position in place. Ideally, the photocopy should rest against the glass without need of glue or tape for reinforcement.

2 Heat the gel in a pan over low heat to the highest temperature recommended by the manufacturer. Fill the container with gel and arrange the wick. Carefully remove as many bubbles as possible by gently stirring the gel with the bubble stick. Place the candle in the refrigerator for several hours to solidify.

Designer: **Megan Kirby**

Designer Tip: *An excess of bubbles can ruin the effect of your photo or patterned background. To remove bubbles from the finished candle, place the candle in the oven at 175°F (79°C) for several hours. Stir the gel with the bubble stick and put the candle in the refrigerator again to cool. Because the paper background can cause an outpouring of bubbles, you may need to repeat this process several times.*

Safety Note: *Never allow a gel candle to burn unattended.*

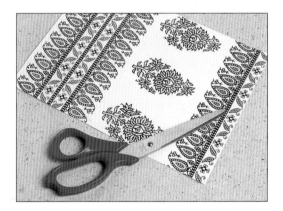

Gift
Candles

Gel candles may well be the ideal gift

because they're so easy to customize

for the recipient. Looking for a small

hostess gift? Just tint a batch of gel to

match her favorite table setting or

couch pillow. Have a friend who's cele-

brating a special occasion? Search out

symbolic (and nonflammable) items

that can be embedded in a candle for a

special gift. Add their favorite fragrance

or chose a container that's special or

unique for a one-of-a-kind gift.

Gel Candle Wall Display

*B*old lines of the wire and the ruffled look of the silk carnation seen through the clear gel make this wall design both daring and romantic. A matching table centerpiece would coordinate all the candlelight in the room. To set an after-dinner mood, scent with sandalwood or jasmine. Then turn on the music...

MATERIALS

- Clip-on pan thermometer
- Pan
- Votive candle wall display with glass candle containers
- Candle gel
- Wick
- Stem of silk flowers and foliage
- Wire cutters
- Metal skewer

INSTRUCTIONS

1 Heat the gel in a pan over low heat to the highest temperature recommended by the manufacturer. While the gel is melting, trim a flower or a leaf for each of your glass containers.

2 Transfer a small amount of melted gel to a smaller pot and drop the silk flowers and leaves into the pan. Stir them into the gel so that all areas are covered.

3 Position a flower or leaf at the bottom of each candle container. Pour the gel from the larger pan over them, then use the metal skewer to fine-tune their placement. Position the wicks in place and allow the gel to solidify undisturbed for several hours.

Designers: **Dawn Cusick** *and* **Theresa Gwynn**

Safety Note: *Do not burn the wick within an inch (2.5cm) of silk blooms or foliage.*

Prosperity Goblet

Spangles shaped like ancient coins glitter in a goblet filled with emerald green gel. Both the gold coins and the color green are ancient symbols of prosperity, making this a perfect gift for a friend starting a new job or going into an entrepreneurial venture. Every time the candle is lit, your good wishes will glow with it.

INSTRUCTIONS

1 Melt a small amount of gel in a pan. Place the coins in the gel and watch for bubbles. If no bubbles appear, use tweezers to remove the coins, holding them over the pan until the gel solidifies. If the coins bubble, leave them in the gel until they stop bubbling, stirring occasionally.

2 String each coin a length of sewing thread. Suspend the coins around the edges of the container and secure by taping the strings in place.

3 Melt enough gel to fill the container over low heat to the highest temperature recommended by the manufacturer. Pour the gel over the coins and arrange the wick. Allow the candle to cool undisturbed in the refrigerator for several hours.

4 Remove the strings from the finished candle by gently pulling on them.

Note: If your finished candle has more bubbles in it than you like, place it in a 175°F (79°C) oven for several hours, then stir out any remaining bubbles with the bubble stick and cool again in the refrigerator.

Designer: **Megan Kirby** *(left and right)*

MATERIALS

- Clip-on pan thermometer
- Pan
- Green glass container
- 10 to 12 jewelry coins (with small, predrilled holes) or coinlike buttons
- Sewing thread
- Candle gel
- Wick
- Bubble stick

VARIATION

For a going-away gift, make a gel candle with a small ceramic cat waving good-bye. The cat is sitting on a bed of red heart beads.

Fresh Flower Candles

Fire and water do mix! Fresh flowers are in a water bath on the bottom—and firelight comes from colored gel in a separate container on top. This two-part hors d'oeuvre container surrounds shrimp with ice to keep it cold. For candles, fill the bottom with water, or leave it empty—and you can use fresh flowers, herbs, real fruit, silk ribbons—anything that can't be put directly in the gel—and keep it safe and fresh. Lovely!

MATERIALS

- Clip-on pan thermometer
- Pan
- Two-piece nesting container
- Candle gel
- Gel dye
- Wick
- Fresh flowers

INSTRUCTIONS

1 Melt the gel in a pan over low heat until it reaches the highest temperature recommended by the manufacturer. Pour the gel into the top container and position the wick. Allow the gel to solidify undisturbed in the refrigerator for several hours.

2 Add a small amount of water to the bottom container and float a fresh-cut flower in it.

Designer: **Dawn Cusick**

VARIATION

Trim the stem from a silk flower and place it in a small amount of gel until it stops bubbling. Remove the flower and place it in the bottom of a container, then pour gel over it and position a wick.

Faux Fruit Cocktail

This cheery candle will keep your guests guessing! The fruit is really chunks of colorful candle wax cut to look like pineapple and watermelon. Scenting will increase the fruity impression.

INSTRUCTIONS

1 Arrange a selection of wax chunks in the bottom of your container. *(Note: Lighter colors tend to work better than darker ones.)* Pinks, reds, and oranges were used here because of their resemblance to fruit.

2 Heat the gel in a pan over low heat to the highest temperature recommended by the manufacturer. Remove the pan from the heat and allow the gel to cool about 50 degrees F (10°C). Pour the gel over the wax chunks, allowing some of the chunks on the top layer to protrude out from the gel. Position the wick and refrigerate the candle.

Designer: **Megan Kirby** *(left and right)*

VARIATION

Line the bottom of an antique jam jar with several layers of small blue marbles and pour lightly tinted blue gel over them. Add a wick and enjoy!

Cherry Parfait

Bright red glass cherries in a jar of pink-tinted gel are like goodies at the bottom of an ice cream sundae! Use this candle as a sweet touch on a kitchen counter or as a capricious accent on pantry shelves. Other options are berries (marbles) in blue gel or peaches (wax chunks) in pale orange gel.

INSTRUCTIONS

1 Melt the gel in a pan over low heat until it reaches the highest temperature recommended by the manufacturer. Add just enough red dye to lightly tint the gel. (Doublecheck the color by removing a small amount of gel on a spoon and placing it on a sheet of heavy white paper.) Add additional gel to the pan if the color is too dark or additional dye if it's too light.

2 Melt a small amount of gel in a second pan. Place the cherries in the gel and watch for bubbles. If no bubbles appear, use tweezers to remove the cherries by their stems, holding them over the pan until the gel covering them solidifies. If the cherries do bubble, leave them in the gel until the bubbling stops, stirring occasionally.

3 Arrange the cherries in the bottom of the container and pour the tinted gel over them. Arrange the wick and stir the gel slowly in a swirling pattern with the bubble stick. Allow to cool undisturbed for several hours in the refrigerator.

Note: If your finished candle has more bubbles in it than you like, place it in a 175°F (79°C) oven for several hours, then stir out any remaining bubbles with the bubble stick and cool again in the refrigerator.

Designer: **Megan Kirby**

MATERIALS

- Clip-on pan thermometer
- Pan
- Candy container with lid
- 4 glass cherries with stems
- Candle gel
- Gel dye
- Wick
- Tweezers
- Bubble stick

Friendly Sharks

Sharks are friendly in this aquamarine-tinted gel candle. Other sea creatures that look swimmingly good in gel candles are dolphins, goldfish, starfish, and squiggly octopuses. Add green ribbon for a seaweed effect.

MATERIALS

- Clip-on pan thermometer
- Pan
- Glass container
- 2 glass sharks
- Beach sand
- Sewing thread
- Candle gel
- Gel dye
- Wick
- Bubble stick

INSTRUCTIONS

1 Melt a small amount of gel in a small pan. Place the sharks in the gel and watch for bubbles. If no bubbles appear, use tweezers to remove the sharks by the tips of their tails, holding them over the pan until the gel solidifies. If the sharks do bubble, leave them in the gel until they stop bubbling, stirring occasionally.

2 Line the bottom of your container with beach sand. Place one of the sharks directly on the sand near the sides of the glass. Suspend the second shark over two pieces of thread halfway up the container and secure by taping the strings in place.

3 Melt enough gel to fill the container over low heat until it reaches 210°F. Add just enough blue and green dye to lightly tint the gel a pale turquoise. (Doublecheck the color by removing a small amount of gel on a spoon and placing it on a sheet of heavy white paper.) Add additional gel to the pan if the color is too dark or additional dye if it's too light.

4 Pour the gel over the sharks and arrange the wick. Allow the candle to cool undisturbed in the refrigerator for several hours. *Note: If your finished candle has more bubbles in it than you like, place it in a 175°F (79°C) oven for several hours, then stir out any remaining bubbles with the bubble stick and cool again in the refrigerator.*

5 Remove the strings from the finished candle by gently pulling on them.

Designer: **Megan Kirby**

Personal Bath Candles

Because gel candles are so easy to make, you can now have candles tinted to match your bathroom décor and scented exactly the way you want them. Even better, you can have bath candle containers that are yours and yours alone—gifts from loved ones, travel souvenirs, and flea market treasures.

MATERIALS

- Clip-on pan thermometer
- Pan
- Small glass containers or soap dishes
- Candle gel
- Wick
- Gel dye

INSTRUCTIONS

1 Melt the gel in a pan over low heat to the highest temperature recommended by the manufacturer. Add small amounts of dye until you're happy with the color. (Doublecheck the color by removing a small amount of gel on a spoon and placing it on a sheet of heavy white paper.) Add additional gel to the pan if the color is too dark or additional dye if it's too light. Position the wick and allow the candles to cool undisturbed for several hours.

Designer: **Chris Rankin** *(left and right)*

Safety Note: *Be sure to note the information on page 13 about adding fragrance to gel candles.*

VARIATION

Stir in a small amount of a refreshing fragrance oil just before you pour the candle. Make several extra to have on hand for impromptu gift-giving.

Beaded Candles

Beads in ancient colors of amber, amethyst and gold...a heavy goblet reminiscent of Roman glass.... When the candle is lit, the beads glow eerily like treasures lost in time.

INSTRUCTIONS

1 Make a small loop at one end of the wire, then string the beads. Place the strung beads in the container and bend the wire to follow the curves of the container until you are happy with the look. Trim off any excess wire and make a small loop at the other end of the wire.

2 Melt a small amount of gel in a small pan. Remove the strung beads from the container and place them in the gel and watch for bubbles. If no bubbles appear, use tweezers to remove the beads by one of the wire loops, holding them over the pan until the gel solidifies. If the gel around the beads bubbles, leave the beads in the gel until the bubbling stops, stirring occasionally. Replace the beads in the glass container.

3 Melt the gel over low heat to the highest temperature recommended by the manufacturer, then pour over the beads. Arrange the wick and stir the gel slowly in a swirling pattern with the bubble stick. Allow to cool undisturbed for several hours in the refrigerator. *Note: If your finished candle has more bubbles in it than you like, place it in a 175°F (79°C) oven for several hours, then stir out any remaining bubbles with the bubble stick and cool again in the refrigerator.*

Designers: **Terry Taylor** (left) and **Theresa Gwynn** (right)

MATERIALS

- Clip-on pan thermometer
- Pan
- Glass container with varying contours
- Assortment of colorful beads
- 20-inch (50 cm) length of medium-gauge wire
- Wire cutters
- Candle gel
- Wick
- Metal skewer
- Bubble stick

VARIATION

String two lengths of glass beads on sewing thread and suspend them in a container. Secure the strings on the outside of the container with tape, then pour the gel and position the wick. Gently remove the strings after the gel has solidified.

Sand and Gel Candles

Ultracontemporary, bold and fun, these sand-and-gel layered candles grab attention in any decor. The colored sand provides easy color to contrast with the gel. Paint the glasses in any wild colors that strike your fancy.

MATERIALS

- Clip-on pan thermometer
- Pan
- Specialty glassware with multiple sections
- Craft sand
- Candle gel
- Wick

INSTRUCTIONS

1 Melt a small amount of gel in a pan to the highest temperature recommended by the manufacturer. Carefully pour the gel into the bottom section of the glass. Place the glass in the refrigerator and allow to completely solidify. *(Note: If you try to rush the process, the bottom layer of the gel will sag from the weight of the sand, so be sure to allow the first layer of gel to completely harden before moving on.)*

2 Carefully check the inside of your glass to make sure that you haven't accidentally spilled any gel there. If so, remove it completely before continuing. Fill the third section of the glass with a layer of gel and add the wick.

Designer: **Theresa Gwynn** *(left and right)*

VARIATION

Thinner layers of gel and sand can be used to create different effects. For best results, be sure to check the interior of the container for spilled gel before adding new layers of sand.

Nuts n' Bolts Gel Candle

Even unlit, this "hardware" candle will sparkle on the workshop shelves of your favorite handyperson. Use it as a gift to lighten up the reception of your next "honey-do" list!

INSTRUCTIONS

1 String the larger hardware items on a length of sewing thread. Suspend them in the container and secure by taping the string in place.

2 Place the container in a 175°F (79°C) oven. In a pan, melt enough gel to fill the container over low heat until it reaches the highest temperature recommended by the manufacturer.

3 Remove the container from the oven. Pour the liquid gel in the container and arrange a wick. Reposition the hardware items with the metal skewer if desired. Stir the gel gently in a swirling pattern with the bubble stick, then place the candle in the refrigerator for several hours to cool.

4 Remove the strings from the finished candle by gently pulling on them.

Note: If your finished candle has more bubbles in it than you like, place it in a 175°F (79°C) oven for several hours, then stir out any remaining bubbles with the bubble stick and cool again in the refrigerator.

Designer: **Theresa Gwynn**

MATERIALS

- Clip-on pan thermometer
- Pan
- Glass container
- Assortment of hardware items in varying shapes and sizes
- Candle gel
- Tweezers
- Sewing thread
- Wick
- Metal skewer
- Bubble stick

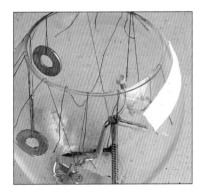

Sweet Dreams Scented Candles

*W*hat a welcome message this scented duo offers to houseguests weary from travel. As a unique gift for the new baby, tint them pink or blue.

INSTRUCTIONS

1 String the letters to spell out the words "sweet" and "dreams" on separate strands of sewing thread. Suspend the letters in the containers and secure by taping the strings in place.

2 Melt the gel in a pan over low heat until it reaches the highest temperature recommended by the manufacturer. Add just enough dye to lightly tint the gel. Doublecheck the color by removing a small amount of gel on a spoon and placing it on a sheet of heavy white paper. Add additional gel to the pan if the color is too dark or additional dye if it's too light. Stir in several drops of lavender essential oil.

3 Melt a small amount of gel in a second pan. Place the lambs in the gel and watch for bubbles. If no bubbles appear, use tweezers to remove the lambs by the narrow part of their legs, holding them over the pan until the gel covering them solidifies. If the lambs do bubble, leave them in the gel until they stop bubbling, stirring occasionally.

4 Position the lambs in the bottom of the containers and pour the gel over them. Arrange the wick and allow the candles to cool several hours in the refrigerator.

5 Remove the strings from the finished candle by gently pulling on them.

Designer: **Megan Kirby**

MATERIALS

- Clip-on pan thermometer
- Pan
- 2 glass containers
- Letter beads
- Sewing thread
- 2 ceramic lambs
- Candle gel
- Gel dye
- Lavender essential oil
- Wick
- Tweezers
- Bubble stick

T-Rex and Friends Gel Candle

Kids get a big kick out of this candle with diminutive metal dinosaurs. Let them design their own candles from what they'll pull from their secret treasure boxes...bracelet charms, toy soldiers, Monopoly game pieces, tiny space aliens, your old earrings...

MATERIALS

o Clip-on pan thermometer
o Pan
o Green craft sand
o Metal dinosaur figures (sold at toy and miniature stores)
o Candle gel
o Wick

INSTRUCTIONS

1 Line the bottom of your container with a layer of green craft sand. (If you'd like a lighter colored sand, dilute with ordinary beach sand. Remember, the sand color will look darker after gel is poured over it.) Arrange the dinosaurs in the sand until you're happy with the look, then arrange the sand so that it looks like rolling hills.

2 Heat the gel in a pan over low heat to the highest temperature recommended by the manufacturer. Carefully pour the gel over the sand and position the wick.

Note: If your finished candle has too many bubbles in it, refer to the instructions of pages 14 and 15 for removing bubbles from a finished candle.

Designer: **Theresa Gwynn**

Safety Note: *Remember to trim your wick to ¹/₄ inch (6 mm) after every use.*

Moroccan Tea Glass Candles

Pretty containers like these Moroccan tea glasses are so attractive by themselves, there is no need to color the gel. Add your favorite scent to increase the exotic appeal. Group displays like this one are, of course, dramatic. But any good-looking glass can be filled with gel and become a stand-alone beauty.

MATERIALS

- Clip-on pan thermometer
- Pan
- Set of Moroccan tea glasses
- Candle gel
- Wick
- Fragrance oil

INSTRUCTIONS

1 Melt the gel in a pan over low heat to the highest temperature recommended by the manufacturer. Carefully stir in 1 or 2 drops of fragrance oil for each candle, then pour the gel into the glasses. (Review the Fragrance section on page 13 for tips about what types of fragrance oil to use and how to prevent cloudy gel.)

Designer: **Terry Taylor**

Introduce a hint of the exotic to your home by scenting *your candles with the fragrances of Morocco. Cedarwood, cypress, frankinsence, myrrh, rose, jasmine, neroli (orange blossom) and citron (Moroccan lime) are all aromatics derived from North African and Mediterranean basin plants. And what could be more fitting than to scent your tea glasses with peppermint, in homage to that most commonplace of moroccan beverages, green mint tea?*

Safety Note: *Be sure to note the information on page 13 about adding fragrance to gel candles.*

Celebration
Candles

Brighten your holidays and special occasions with the glowing light and style of gel candles. The excitement of upcoming celebrations can release waves of creativity that will amaze you. Review the Special Effects section on pages 12 and 13 if you need a few ideas to get started, then break out the glitter, holiday ornaments, and your most unusual containers.

Happy Birthday Cake Candle

Make a secret wish and blow out the candles, but don't count the calories—the frothy-looking delights on this birthday cake candle are whipped gel, not sugar! To make it extra special, paint the lucky birthday person's name on the glass and decorate with stick-on glitter stars.

MATERIALS

- Clip-on pan thermometer
- Pan
- Cake-shaped glass container
- Candle gel
- Gel dye
- White crayon
- Butter knife
- Birthday candles

INSTRUCTIONS

1 Melt enough gel to fill most of the glass container in a pan at the highest temperature recommended by the manufacturer. Add just enough dye to tint the gel a pale pink. Doublecheck the color by removing a small amount of gel on a spoon and placing it on a sheet of heavy white paper. Add additional gel to the pan if the color is too dark or additional dye if it's too light.

2 Heat the container in a 175°F (79°C) oven for 10 minutes, then pour a layer of pink gel into the container. Place the container in the refrigerator until it completely solidifies. Save the remaining tinted gel.

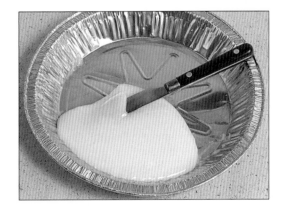

3 Heat a small amount of gel until it first begins to melt. Add several white crayon shavings to the gel and stir well to create a frothy, frosting effect. Pour a thin layer of this gel over the pink layer and allow to solidify completely.

4 Reheat the leftover gel from Step 2, then remove the pan from the heat. Fold the gel over the surface of a butter knife repeatedly until the gel becomes opaque. Pour the gel over the middle frosting layer and allow to completely solidify.

5 Repeat Step 3 and use it to "frost" the cake. Allow this layer to harden for a few minutes, then insert the candles.

Designer: **Megan Kirby**

Martini Candle

This Martini Candle is a real icebreaker for strangers at a party bar! Display with other cocktail variations...use red gel and a celery stick for a Bloody Mary...lime colored gel and a mint leaf for a Grasshopper...or go really wild with light orange gel for a Mai Tai, topped with a cherry, a tiny purple orchid, and a paper umbrella!

MATERIALS

- Clip-on pan thermometer
- Pan
- Martini glass
- Large olive
- Large toothpick
- Candle gel
- Wick
- Bubble stick

INSTRUCTIONS

1 Insert the toothpick into the olive at an angle and place it in the bottom of the martini glass.

2 Heat enough gel to fill the glass in a pan over low heat. Pour the gel over the olive and arrange the wick. Remember, pouring the gel as soon as it melts will give you more bubbles; pouring at a hotter temperature will give you fewer bubbles.

Designers: **Dawn Cusick** *(left) and* **Terry Taylor** *(right)*

Safety Note: *Do not allow the wick to burn within 1 inch (2.5 cm) of the olive.*

VARIATION

For a different look, replace the martini glass with a drinking glass and the olive with a decorative swizzle stick.

Easter Candles

Spring has come at last! Make it official with a pair of blossom-colored, giant egg candles. Display them with painted Easter eggs and jelly beans in a nest of pastel ribbons.

MATERIALS

- Clip-on pan thermometer
- Pan
- Egg-shaped container
- Gel dye
- Wick
- Bubble stick

INSTRUCTIONS

1 Melt enough gel to fill about half the container in a pan over low heat until it reaches the highest temperature recommended by the manufacturer. Add just enough dye to lightly tint the gel a spring color. Doublecheck the color by removing a small amount of gel on a spoon and placing it on a sheet of heavy white paper. Add additional gel to the pan if the color is too dark or additional dye if it's too light.

2 Pour the gel into the container. Gently stir the gel with the bubble stick in a swirling pattern. Place the container in the refrigerator and allow the gel to solidify.

3 Repeat Steps 1 and 2 with a second color of tinted gel for the candle on the left and add the wick. For the candle on the right, create two frothy layers by using a butter knife to fold the gel over on itself in the pan as it cools. (See page 13 for a review of the technique.)

Designer: **Megan Kirby**

VARIATION

For a stained-glass effect, fill a container with scrap pieces of tinted gel, then pour gel over them and add a wick. To prevent the colors from bleeding, allow the melted gel to cool for several minutes before pouring.

Insect-Repellent Gel Candles

These whimsical bug candles add an entertaining entomological buzz to your summer picnic table. With a drop of citronella, they're beneficial, too—by keeping real bugs away!

INSTRUCTIONS

1 Melt a small amount of gel in a pan. Place the bugs in the gel and watch for bubbles. If no bubbles appear, use tweezers to remove the bugs one at a time, holding each one over the pan until the gel solidifies. If you do see bubbles around the bugs, leave them in the gel until they stop bubbling, stirring occasionally.

2 Melt enough gel to fill the containers over low heat until the gel reaches the highest temperature recommended by the manufacturer. Stir in 3 drops of essential oil for each candle you plan to make. Pour the liquid gel over the bugs, then use the metal skewer to rearrange the bugs if desired.

3 Place the wicks. Gently swirl the gel with the bubble stick to remove as many bubbles as possible, then place in the refrigerator for several hours to solidify.

Designer: **Dawn Cusick**

MATERIALS

- Clip-on pan thermometer
- Pan
- Small glass containers
- Colorful, plastic or ceramic bugs
- Candle gel
- Tweezers
- Citronella essential oil
- Metal skewer
- Wick
- Bubble stick

VARIATION

For the entomology hobbyist, place a large, interesting bug (already dead, of course) in a small container and cover with gel.

Winter Holiday Globe Candle

Holiday ornaments seem to float on winter's wind in this Santa-size globe candle. For a festive centerpiece, frame it with brilliant red berries or nestle it on a bed of evergreens. For Valentine's Day, fill it with shiny red glass hearts. For Halloween, tint it orange to go with grinning ceramic jack-o'-lanterns.

MATERIALS

- Clip-on pan thermometer
- Pan
- Globe-shaped container
- Green glitter
- Christmas ornaments
- Sewing thread
- Candle gel
- Wick
- Bubble stick

INSTRUCTIONS

1 Melt a small amount of gel in a small pan. Place the ornaments in the gel and watch for bubbles. If no bubbles appear, use tweezers to remove the ornaments by their hangers, holding them over the pan until the gel solidifies. If the ornaments do bubble, leave them in the gel until they stop bubbling, stirring occasionally.

2 Line the bottom of the container with a layer of green glitter. String the ornaments on a length of sewing thread. Suspend the ornaments in the container and secure by taping the string in place.

3 Melt enough gel to fill the container over low heat to the highest temperature recommended by the manufacturer. Pour the gel over the ornaments and arrange the wick. Allow the candle to cool undisturbed in the refrigerator for several hours.

4 Remove the string from the finished candle by gently pulling on them.

Designers: **Theresa Gwynn** *(left)* and **Terry Taylor** *(right)*

VARIATION

For this candle, small angel ornaments were added to the poured gel after the gel had begun to thicken.

Glow-in-the-Dark Gel Candles

*C*reate instant chemistry by adding phosphorescent pigment powder to your gel candle. The candle will absorb surrounding light and glow softly in any darkened room.

MATERIALS

- Clip-on pan thermometer
- Pan
- Graduated cylinder or beaker
- Candle gel
- Phosphorescent pigment
- Wick
- Bubble stick

INSTRUCTIONS

1 Melt a small amount of gel in a pan over low heat to the highest temperature recommended by the manufacturer. Stir in a small amount of glow-in-the-dark pigment (2% pigment, 98% gel is the recommended amount) just before pouring and stir well.

2 Stir the gel in a swirling pattern with the bubble stick to keep the pigment particles from accumulating on the bottom. Add a wick and place the candle in the refrigerator to cool.

Designers: **Katye Herron, The Chemistry Store** *(left) and* **Megan Kirby** *(right)*

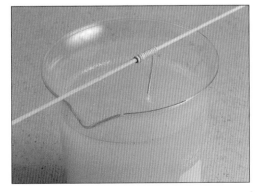

VARIATION

Fill a chemistry beaker with gel that's been tinted a rich, blue-green color.

Safety Note: *Never allow a gel candle to burn unattended.*

Patriotic Gel Candles

Easy-to-make candles glow with patriotic pride to celebrate Fourth of July, Election Day or "Welcome Home from Boot Camp!" When lit, they flicker in red, white, and blue. Use other color variations as welcoming décor for foreign visitors. Red and white with a maple leaf for Canada. Green, white, and orange for Ireland—with an unofficial but perfectly appropriate shamrock!

INSTRUCTIONS

1 Melt a small amount of gel in a pan over low heat to the highest temperature recommended by the manufacturer. Tint the gel blue, adding the pigment in small quantities until you've achieved the perfect color. (Tip: To find out exactly how your blue gel will look, place a tablespoon of the tinted gel on a piece of heavy white paper.) Pour the blue gel into the bottom third of each glass. Allow the gel to completely solidify (approximately 2 hours).

2 Clean your melting pan, taking care to remove all traces of the red gel. Melt another small batch of gel and pour it into the middle third of the glasses. Allow the gel to sit for 2 minutes, then place a star in each glass and guide it into an upright position with the metal skewer. Allow the gel to completely solidify.

3 Repeat Step 1 for the top third of the glasses, this time tinting the gel red.

Designer: **Megan Kirby**

Safety Note: *Remember to trim your wick to 1/4 inch (6 mm) after every use.*

MATERIALS

- Clip-on pan thermometer
- Pan
- 2 clear glass drinking glasses
- Candle gel
- Wick
- Red and blue gel dyes
- 2 gold stars, approximately 2 inches (5 cm) tall
- Metal skewer

Bubbly Beer Mug Candle

The bubbles in this clever candle are warm eye catchers for cold-beer drinkers! Display several on an Oktoberfest buffet. For special "brewmeisters," use bottle tops of their favorite beer.

MATERIALS

o Clip-on pan thermometer
o Pan
o Tall beer mug
o Assortment of colorful beer tops
o Glue gun and glue
o Candle gel
o Gel dye
o Wick
o Metal skewer
o White crayon (optional)

INSTRUCTIONS

1 Attach beer tops to the inside of the beer stein with their emblems facing out.

2 Melt enough gel to fill the mug in a pan over low heat to the highest temperature recommended by the manufacturer. Add just enough yellow dye to lightly tint the gel a pale beer color. (Doublecheck the color by removing a small amount of gel on a spoon and placing it on a sheet of heavy white paper.) Add additional gel to the pan if the color is too dark or additional dye if it's too light. Fill the mug with the gel and arrange the wick, then allow to cool on a countertop.

3 To add a faux head to the candle, add a few shavings from a white crayon to a small amount of melted gel. Stir well and pour over the hardened first layer. Stir with wooden stick or spoon to create bubbles and pour over the hardened layer.

Designer: **Terry Taylor** *(left and right)*

VARIATION

Fill the beer stein with tinted gel, then drop a handful of tops into the gel. Add a frothy head as directed in Step 3.

Champagne Candles

Glowing good cheer from these champagne glass candles will last long past midnight! Paint the year on the glass for New Year's Eve. Add glittery color ribbons to accentuate the festive mood.

MATERIALS

o Clip-on pan thermometer
o Pan
o Champagne glasses
o Candle gel
o Gel dye
o Wick
o Wood cooking skewer

INSTRUCTIONS

1 Heat the gel in a pan over low heat until it just begins to melt, stirring as little as possible. Add just enough yellow dye to lightly tint the gel a pale champagne color. (Doublecheck the color by removing a small amount of gel on a spoon and placing it on a sheet of heavy white paper.) Add additional gel to the pan if the color is too dark or additional dye if it's too light.

2 Pour the gel into the glasses and arrange the wick. Create extra bubbles by placing the wood skewer in the top $1/4$ inch (3 mm) of the gel and gently moving the skewer.

Designer: **Dawn Cusick** *(left and right)*

Safety Note: *Do not allow the wick to burn within 1 inch (2.5 cm) of the bottom of the container.*

VARIATION

Decorate a champagne gel candle with white flowers and ribbons for a special wedding gift.

Anniversary Swans Candle

Because they mate for life and live a long time, swans are timeless symbols of love. In this graceful glass, layers of colored gel lie on a bed of "pearls" while two swans swim in the same direction.

MATERIALS

- Clip-on pan thermometer
- Pan
- Large wineglass
- Small craft pearls
- Candle gel
- Gel dye
- 2 ceramic or metal swans
- Sewing thread
- Tweezers
- Wick
- Bubble stick

INSTRUCTIONS

1 Line the bottom of the glass with a thin layer of craft pearls. Melt a small amount of gel to the highest temperature recommended by the manufacturer and tint it a pale green. Pour the gel over the pearls. Place the glass in the refrigerator until the gel solidifies.

2 Melt a small amount of untinted gel in a pan. Place the swans in the gel and watch for bubbles. If no bubbles appear, use tweezers to remove the swans from the gel and hold them over the pan until the gel solidifies. If the swans do bubble, leave them in the gel until they stop bubbling, stirring occasionally.

3 Suspend the swans in the container with strings so they appear to be swimming on the green layer and secure by taping the strings in place.

4 Melt another batch of gel to the highest temperature recommended by the manufacturer and tint it to a pale pink. Doublecheck the color by removing a small amount of gel on a spoon and placing it on a sheet of heavy white paper. Add additional gel to the pan if the color is too dark or additional dye if it's too light.

5 Fill the remainder of the glass with pink gel and arrange the wick. Remove as many bubbles as possible by swirling the gel with the bubble stick. Place the candle in the refrigerator for several hours to solidify. Remove the strings from the finished candle.

Designer: **Megan Kirby**

Index

Acknowledgments

The author would like to thank the following companies and individuals for their numerous contributions to this book:

Yaley Enterprises of Redding, California, for gel donations and technical assistance;

Photographers Evan Bracken and Richard Hasselberg, for their excellent photography;

The Chemistry Store (www.chemistrystore.com), a shop specializing in products used to design gel candles and other crafts for the hobbyist, student, and industry, for providing glow-in-the-dark pigment;

and designers Katye Herron, Theresa Gwynn, Terry Taylor, Megan Kirby, and Dawn Cusick for so generously sharing their gel candle creations and techniques.